Series Editors:

Laure Mistral
Philippe Godard

Also Available:

We Live in India
We Live in China
We Live in Brazil

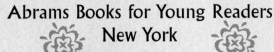

We Live in
Japan

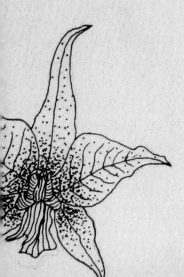

Alexandre Messager

Illustrations by Sophie Duffet

Abrams Books for Young Readers
New York

CHINA

RUSSIA
(SIBERIA)

HOKKAIDO

Sapporo

NORTH
KOREA

氣

HONSHU

SOUTH
KOREA

JAPAN

Tokyo

Yokohama

Kyoto
Nagoya

Hiroshima

Kobe

Kitakyushu

Osaka

Fukuoka

SHIKOKU

Nagasaki

KYUSHU

Presenting . . . Japan!

Japan is a country of more than 6,800 islands that stretches 2,300 miles across the sea. These islands are actually the summits of a long chain of underwater volcanic mountains that rise above the surface of the ocean. Because of this, 70 percent of the land is mountainous. The highest peak is the volcano Mount Fuji (*Fujiyama* or *Fuji-san*), which reaches an altitude of 12,388 feet. Ninety-six percent of the Japanese population lives on one of the four main islands: Honshu, Shikoku, Kyushu, and Hokkaido.

Surface Area: Japan covers an area of 145,882 square miles (99 percent land, 1 percent water), which is about the size of Montana.

Population: In 2005, Japan's population was estimated to be 127.5 million. The population density is one of the highest in the world, with 874 people per square mile, much higher than in the United States. Interestingly, Japan has the longest life expectancy in the world. On average, women live to be eighty-five and men live to be seventy-eight.

Official Language: Japanese.

Major Religions: Approximately 84 percent of Japanese practice both Shinto and Buddhism. Less than 1 percent of the population practices Christianity.

Major Cities: Japan is an urban society. Some cities are so large that they touch; these are called conurbations. For example, Tokyo, the most populated city in the world, has merged into Yokohama; 33.4 million people live in the Tokyo-Yokohama conurbation.

Climate: Like the United States, Japan has a temperate climate, with four distinct seasons.

Earthquakes, Tsunamis, and Typhoons: There are often earthquakes in Japan. Depending upon their intensity, earthquakes can cause tidal waves, which are called tsunamis. Each September near the end of the month, there is also a period of strong winds, which are called typhoons. These storms often cause enormous amounts of damage.

Legendary Beginnings

Japan, or the Land of the Rising Sun, is an archipelago composed of thousands of islands that, according to legend, were created by the goddess Izanami. One day, she plunged her spear into the ocean. When she pulled it out, the drops of water that fell from the spear became islands, forming Japan.

No one knows the exact origins of the Japanese people. The first inhabitants of the archipelago were the Ainu, the people who now live in the north of the country, on the island of Hokkaido.

For most of its history, Japan has been an isolated country. For a long time, China and Korea were its only links with the outside world. This isolation was a result of its geographical situation. Japan established trade links with China very early on, in 57 BCE. Chinese culture has thus greatly influenced Japanese culture. It was only in the 1540s that the first Western ships, belonging to Portuguese traders, sailed into Japanese ports. At this point in history, the Portuguese were the world's greatest sailors. They had already made contact with a number of Asian countries, in particular Indonesia, in order buy spices. But Japan's emperor reacted immediately to the intrusion of Portuguese ships in Japanese waters: He closed all ports and forbade the Japanese to leave their islands, in order to prevent the strangers from exerting even the slightest influence on the country. Then, in 1639, under pressure from the Japanese lords (the shogun), who were afraid of losing their power, Japan closed its borders entirely to foreigners.

It was only in 1853, following the sudden emergence of the United States Navy on its coast, that Japan reopened to the world. The Meiji emperor, who wanted to modernize Japanese society and feared that his country was lagging behind the rest of the world, decided that it was time to take stock of what exactly the West could offer Japan. Japanese people were sent to Europe and America to learn more about the best aspects of Western civilization. After just a few years, Japanese society was completely transformed. In 1905, their victory over Russia in the Russo-Japanese War proved that Japan had become a world power.

At the beginning of World War II, Japan was neutral. However, Germany's success encouraged them to become more aggressive. Beginning with a surprise attack on Pearl Harbor, the U.S. naval base in the Pacific Ocean, Japan proceeded to invade a number of Asian countries. It was only in 1945, after atomic bombs were dropped on Hiroshima and Nagasaki, that Japan finally surrendered. Japan has never again had an army. However, in 2004, a contingent of the Japan Self-Defense Forces was sent to Iraq to help U.S. troops.

Japan changed completely following World War II. The Japanese rebuilt their war-torn country and developed big industries, manufacturing cars, boats, trains, televisions, computers, video games, and electronics. Today, it has become an industrial power that exerts an economic and cultural supremacy over a large part of the world. Japan is the country with the world's fastest trains (the *Shinkansen*), and it is where the Internet is the most developed. But this ultramodern country has kept a number of its old traditions very much alive.

Aoki, Hayo, and Kenji Invite You to Visit Japan

These three children live on Honshu, the main island of the archipelago.

Aoki lives in Tokyo, the capital of Japan, in a building located in the Minato ward, right in the heart of downtown. Once a year, she goes on vacation to visit her aunt in Sapporo, a city on the island of Hokkaido in the north of Japan. Hokkaido is where the first inhabitants of the archipelago lived.

Hayo lives in Kyoto, the imperial city. He knows a lot about the history of his country. He especially loves the medieval period—the age of the samurai. His mother is a specialist in ikebana (the art of flower arranging) and the tea ceremony. She teaches these traditions to Ogino, Hayo's sister, so that she can continue them. Hayo dreams of becoming a *sumotori*, a sumo wrestler.

Kenji lives in Hiroshima, in a small building near the port. The city of Hiroshima is known throughout the world because it is the first city in history to have been devastated by an atomic bomb, on August 6, 1945. Every year at school, Kenji remembers Sadako Sasaki, a heroine of this terrible tragedy.

Aoki Lives in Tokyo

Aoki was born eleven years ago in Tokyo, the capital of Japan. She lives in a ten-story building in the Minato ward, in the heart of the city. There are many offices, hotels, and businesses in this area.

Tokyo is a megalopolis, a mega-city! It is the most populated city in the world, with more than 30 million residents. It would take Aoki years and years to explore every street and alleyway. Though Japan is very small compared to the United States, it has a large population of nearly 128 million—more people than Mexico!

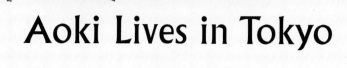

The Different Faces of Tokyo

Tokyo is divided into wards, each with its own characteristics. Shinjuku is one of the most modern wards in Tokyo, with giant neon signs that blink night and day, and enormous television screens on the sides of buildings. There are always throngs of people in the street, and even at night it seems that life there never stops!

The tallest buildings in Tokyo are in Shinjuku, and the headquarters of the most important Japanese companies can be found there. Aoki's father works at an insurance company that has offices on the fifty-fifth floor of one of the buildings. From there, you can admire the views over Tokyo Bay. In Shinjuku, you can also find department stores, restaurants, video arcades, and nightclubs.

The Ueno district, in contrast, is much more traditional and much calmer, with few buildings—it is mostly houses and parks. Last spring, Aoki's class went on a picnic to Ueno Park, which is famous for its blossoming cherry trees. Sometimes you can find futuristic buildings next to Buddhist pagodas or clusters of traditional Japanese wooden houses, all in the same district. It's a little like a village that's tucked away in the middle of a large, modern city.

But Tokyo's strangest feature is in the Aoyama district, close to where Aoki lives: the Tokyo Tower. It's a replica of the Eiffel Tower in Paris and was built in 1958 as a broadcasting antenna for television and radio.

Right next to Tokyo is the city of Yokohama, the largest port in Japan. The two cities are so close that you can't tell where one stops and the other begins. Aoki and her parents often go for walks in Yokohama on the weekends to admire Tokyo Bay and watch the gigantic freighters coming into port. Once or twice a year, Aoki's family gets up very early, at about five o'clock, to go to the all-night fish market there.

Earthquakes

There are often earthquakes in Japan. One popular legend tells of a giant catfish, Namazu, who lives underground and causes earthquakes whenever he moves his tail.

In 1923, Tokyo was devastated by an earthquake that claimed more than 100,000 victims. In 1995, the city of Kobe was also hit by a quake, causing many deaths. Thankfully, major earthquakes like these are rare, and most are not dangerous at all. Furthermore, the Japanese construct buildings with special reinforcements designed to help them endure most tremors. This is effective even when the buildings are very tall.

Sometimes, Aoki and her family are awoken in the middle of the night because the walls and doors are vibrating and the beds are shaking. Most of the time, this lasts only a few seconds, but sometimes it can be really frightening. If the tremors are strong, you have to open a window quickly so that you are able to leave in case the front door gets stuck afterward. Then you should take shelter under a table so you don't get hurt by any falling objects. You should never go outside until the earthquake is over.

Each morning, Aoki walks to school because she's lucky enough to live close by, which isn't the case for many children.

Aoki eats breakfast with her parents, but without her big brother, Shinji. He always wakes up late and often has to run to get to school on time!

Like all Japanese children, Aoki has been going to school since the age of five. She's in the last year of elementary school, which lasts six years. Then, she will go to middle school, where she will begin to learn English. Three years later, she will go to high school.

Unlike in the United States, the school year begins in April and ends in March. There are not a lot of holidays, aside from a one-month vacation in summer. Aoki goes to an all-girls school. But in her brother's high school, there are both boys and girls. In Japanese schools, the children all wear uniforms. Boys wear trousers and jackets, while the girls wear skirts with blazers. This is a way to promote equality among the children.

In Aoki's school, as in all Japanese schools, the rules are very strict. Even when she was very young, Aoki learned to greet her sensei (teachers) by bowing before them as a sign of respect. Teachers represent knowledge and wisdom, and it is the custom to always obey them. This is also a way to pay homage to their age: Elders must be respected. Teachers, for their part, are very attentive to their students.

What Aoki likes most at school are the group calisthenics every morning and classes in origami (the art of paper folding), where she learns to fold paper squares into animals, dolls, and boats without using scissors or glue. This is an exercise in precision and skill that demands a lot of concentration.

     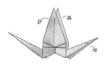

An example of origami

Evening Classes

Beginning in middle school, competition between students becomes fierce, because each one wants to go to the best high schools and universities in the country.

At the end of each academic year, the children take exams. The results of the exams are then evaluated and used to determine which schools they will attend. Students are constantly under pressure. In Japanese schools, there is a common expression: *juken jigoku,* or "examination hell." In Japanese culture, success is extremely important and failure is often still perceived as shameful or dishonorable.

When Aoki comes back home from school in the evening, she sees her brother Shinji for only a couple of minutes. This is because, like many high school students, he goes to a private tutoring school, where he prepares for his exams. These evening classes, called *juku*, are attended by many middle school and high school students who want to prepare for the entrance examinations for the best schools in Tokyo. Next year, when Aoki starts middle school, it will be her turn to go to evening classes.

Before going to see his teacher, Shinji wolfs down a *bento*, a boxed lunch that his mother has made for him. The *bento*, usually served in a small red

box, is very popular in Japan. At any time of day, but particularly at lunch, the Japanese can be seen eating their *bento*. The ubiquitous, tiny red boxes contain different dishes depending on the region. In general, a *bento* includes pieces of chicken or raw fish, and an assortment of cooked and pickled vegetables. Shinji's mother often prepares him a sweet omelette and fish with rice. Shinji eats his dinner very early, because by the time his evening classes are over it is late, and all he wants is to return home and go to bed.

Japanese Writing

At school, Aoki learns how to read and write kanji, the characters used in the Japanese written language.

Spread by Buddhist monks who came to Japan beginning in the fourth century, kanji are complex ideograms (pictures that represent words and phrases), the same as those used in written Chinese. Many of the early characters were originally images or pictures. For example, the word "volcano" is represented by the kanji meaning "fire" placed next to the kanji meaning

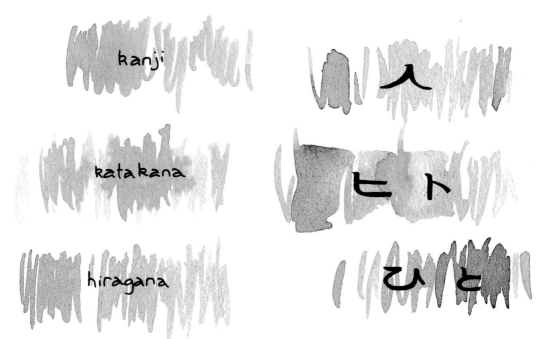

The word "man" written in kanji, katakana, and hiragana

"mountain": Put a fire next to a mountain and you've got a volcano! Aoki already knows five hundred kanji, and by the time she finishes high school, she will know at least two thousand.

But the Japanese writing system is not made up of only kanji. After having temporarily cut off their relations with China around 838, the Japanese invented other symbols that were simpler and better adapted to their way of life. When you look at Japanese writing today, in addition to kanji, you will see other, less complex characters: katakana and hiragana. So in order to write Japanese, you have to use the straight-lined ideograms, kanji, as well as the simpler and more cursive katakana and hiragana.

At school, Aoki first learned hiragana, which are simpler. It was by using these characters that she learned to read and write Japanese. Then her teacher taught her the kanji that are easiest to write and remember. When she goes to middle school, she will learn katakana in addition to other kanji. For now, though, Aoki reads stories written only with hiragana and kanji—specifically *manga*, Japanese comic books.

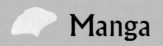# Manga

Like many children her age, Aoki loves to read *manga*, which are easy to understand because of the illustrations and because the writing only uses hiragana.

But *manga* aren't just for children: There are also *manga* for teenagers and even for adults. Aoki's brother and parents read them, too. In Japan, everyone reads *manga*—at home, in the subway, in parks, and even in the street. It's a real cultural phenomenon. There are comic books written about everything!

***Manga* have been popular in Japan** for a very long time. Their popularity first started in 710, when *manga* were rolls of paper (*emakimono*) on which illustrations were drawn together with text. As the paper was unrolled, a story would appear. In the beginning, *manga* were shown only in the emperor's court, before eventually becoming more common. But it was only at the start of the twentieth century that *manga* appeared in their current form, which is like a comic book. Before World War II, the most famous *manga* were *Norakuro* (*The Black Dog*) and *Boken Dankichi* (*The Adventures of Dankichi*). Aoki's grandfather loved these comics, and he gave them to his granddaughter as soon as she could read.

After World War II, *manga* became much more animated, with characters constantly in motion, and very short sentences and words. In 1963, *Tetsuwan Atomu* (*Astro Boy*) became the first televised *manga*, just like *Batman* became a cartoon after starting out as a comic book. Today, there are many *manga* characters on television and in video games.

The Ainu: The First Inhabitants of Japan

Once a year, during summer vacation, Aoki goes to visit her Aunt Kusama, who lives on the island of Hokkaido in Sapporo.

This island is in the far north of Japan, and is close to Russia. Because of snowstorms it gets very cold in winter, but in summer, it is warm and dry. Because of this, many Japanese tourists come here on vacation. Each year, Aoki and her mother fly in a plane over the many mountains and volcanoes near Sapporo. Kusama, Aoki's aunt, was born in Hokkaido and is the ancestor of an Ainu village chief.

Aoki visits the village of Asahikawa, close to Sapporo. It is a reconstructed Ainu village that shows their traditional way of life. Aunt Kusama, who knows the history of the Ainu well, tells how they are considered to be the indigenous inhabitants of the Japanese islands. They came from Siberia, and they have lighter skin than most Japanese people. Several thousand years ago, they settled in Hokkaido, as well as on the neighboring Kuril Islands and the island of Sakhalin, which today belong to Russia.

The Ainu have always tried to maintain their independence. Historically, they were mainly hunters and fishermen. On Hokkaido and in the northern part of Honshu, they built thousands of small villages. But the Ainu were not alone for very long: People from Asia, specifically China and Korea, also began settling on the Japanese archipelago, and little by little they began moving onto the Ainu's land.

In the fifth century, the Ainu were persecuted by the Imperial Court; in the ninth century they were persecuted again by the Fujiwara family. The Fujiwaras were powerful shogun, or military lords. At this point in history they controlled Japan, and they also tried to take control of the Ainu land in the far north. In the nineteenth century, the Japanese government was still trying to expand its territory: This time, they decided to colonize Ainu land and to end their independence once and for all. Major forests were turned into farmland and, deprived of their hunting grounds, many of the Ainu could no longer survive. Those that lived had no choice but to learn how to farm.

Today, there are only a few thousand Ainu left. They are trying to preserve what remains of their cultural heritage. Aunt Kusama, who is Ainu, fought for many years so that the Japanese government would recognize the rights and identity of her people. In 1997, Japan agreed to promote Ainu culture. But this is not enough, and today Aoki's aunt continues to give lectures in Tokyo or Kyoto to talk about her ancestors so that their history is not forgotten. Following Aunt Kusama's example, Aoki has decided to give a presentation on the Ainu when she goes back to school after vacation.

Hayo Lives in Kyoto, the Imperial City

Kyoto was the capital of Japan for a very long time, from 794 to 1868. In fact, in Japanese, "kyoto" means "capital city." Hayo, an eleven-year-old boy, and his sister, Ogino, who is thirteen, live in Kyoto. Their parents run a *ryokan*: a small, traditional inn close to Gion, a historic district.

Like all *ryokan*, the one that belongs to Hayo's family is a large, traditional house that is two stories tall and built entirely of wood. There are fourteen guest rooms, each named after a flower, such as cherry blossom, jasmine, and iris. Next to each guest room, there is also a small sitting room, where guests can drink tea and eat while seated on cushions. But what is really special about a *ryokan* is that you sleep on a futon, a traditional Japanese mattress that is put directly onto the floor and then folded up and put away after you get out of bed. There are two types of beds in Japan: futons and mattresses, like the ones you probably have at home. In Kyoto, the *ryokan* where Hayo and Ogino live is well-known because it is one of the oldest; it has been passed down from generation to generation.

Much smaller than Tokyo, Kyoto is located close to two other large cities, Kobe and Osaka. Together they make up the second-largest conurbation in Japan. Today, Kyoto is well-known because of an important conference that took place there in 1997, during which the Kyoto Protocol, an international treaty to fight global warming and pollution throughout the world, was drawn up.

The city is divided into three major sections: the business district in the south, the old town in the center (where Hayo and Ogino live), and the parks in the north. Even with modernization and the fact that it is no longer the capital of the country, Kyoto remains first and foremost the historic and cultural heart of Japan. The Imperial City's historic monuments were designated UNESCO World Heritage Sites in 1994. Hayo and Ogino are proud to live in such a historic place.

A "Monumental" City

Hayo and Ogino have already visited many of the city's temples and palaces with their families. But there are just as many waiting to be discovered, because there are more than two thousand temples and shrines in all!

Hayo and Ogino are already familiar with the most famous legacies of the imperial past: the emperor's palace; the shogun's palace, which looks like a fortified castle; the Golden Pavilion, whose roof and walls are covered in gold leaf; the Buddhist Temple of the Peaceful Dragon, renowned for its Zen garden of raked sand and rocks, which recalls islands adrift in a sea of waves; and the Silver Pavilion, which has a Chinese-style landscaped garden. During the feudal period, when Japanese society was extremely hierarchal, all of the most prestigious places were reserved for the emperor, the court, the nobility, and the Buddhist monks, who held great power.

Every day in their parents' small hotel, Hayo and Ogino meet new foreign and Japanese tourists who have come to visit the imperial city. Sometimes, their father takes their guests to visit the most famous monuments. He tells them the history of the samurai, who lived in the period when the nobility controlled Japan.

 ## The Shogun and the Samurai

E ver since he was little, Hayo has listened to his father tell the story of the samurai, the most powerful and respected of warriors.

The word "samurai" means "he who serves." These warriors influenced Japanese history from the twelfth century all the way up to the end of the nineteenth century. The time of the samurai began when Japan was divided into shogunates, territories controlled by the lords, or shogun. The shogun were military generals, and they defended their territory with the help of the samurai, formidable warriors who were loyal to their masters until death. But the samurai also served the emperor.

During this long period, there were many battles between shogunates. Some families tried to extend their power, and the samurai fought constantly. The rich samurai fought on horseback; the others fought on foot. The samurai wore helmets designed to frighten their enemies, and their flexible armor was made of thin steel plates that were laced or riveted together. Only the samurai were allowed to use the supreme weapons of war, two swords worn on the left side: the *daito* (a long sword), which was used to fight, and the *shoto* (a short sword), which was used to cut off the head of a defeated samurai. At home, Hayo often dresses up like a samurai. He invites his classmates over, and they stage battles in the garden. Each pretends to be a different shogun, and they take turns dueling.

The Honor Code of the Samurai

Hayo is very familiar with the samurai code.

His father explained to him that under the rule of the shogunates, Japanese society was very hierarchal. Apart from the emperor, who was descended from the gods, the most powerful men were the nobility governing the shogunates. The shogun themselves were placed in a hierarchy according to the amount of territory and money they owned. Then came the craftsmen, the farmers, and the merchants. At the bottom of the ladder were the *eta* (a term now considered extremely derogatory), who did the work that no one else would do.

Samurai held a place of privilege. They didn't have the right to work or earn money; they were required to devote themselves to noble tasks, primarily fighting for their lords. Highly organized, they had a code of conduct and strict rules. A samurai could never hesitate to cut off the head of someone who had acted wrongly toward him, and he needed to be ready to lend his muscle, intelligence, and assets to both the emperor and his master. "To live and die with the sword in hand" was the samurai motto. The greatest dishonor for a samurai was to be taken prisoner. If this happened, he would prefer to commit suicide.

 ## The Art of Flower Arranging

In the inn run by Hayo's parents, each room is decorated with a bouquet of flowers or plants. Some are very simple, others very sophisticated.

In Japan, the art of flower arranging ("ikebana," which literally means "living flowers") is an old tradition that is still popular. Like many Japanese traditions, ikebana was imported from China by Buddhist monks in the seventh century. At this time, floral art was reserved for men. Times have changed, though, because today it is mostly practiced by young girls and women.

Hayo's mother gives classes in flower arranging at the Ikenobo School in Kyoto, the oldest ikebana school in Japan. Hayo's sister, Ogino, spends her time at home trying to arrange flower bouquets, with the help of her mother. Using branches, leaves, and flowers, the object is to create a bouquet that symbolizes heaven, earth, and humankind. Ogino learned to cut the stems under water so that the flowers stay fresh. She also learned to lightly burn or steam the stems to make them stiffer so that the bouquets last longer.

When the end of the year comes, Hayo and Ogino watch their mother prepare dozens of bouquets that are displayed at the entrance to the *ryokan*. For the most part, she uses chrysanthemums and pine branches, because one of the rules of ikebana is to use the plants that best represent the current season. For the Doll Festival (or Girls' Day) in March, Ogino prepares a bouquet with peach or cherry branches. The color and the shape of the vase are also very important, because the vase must match the flowers that are used.

In July, in the Gion district (close to where Hayo's family lives), you can see the most beautiful flower arrangements in Kyoto. It is the biggest festival in the city, and for two days there are parades, floats, and musicians, and many lanterns and floral banners are hung in front of house windows. It is an old festival that dates back to 869, and it is very famous in Japan. It originally served to bring the city's inhabitants together to fight a plague that was ravaging Kyoto and the surrounding towns. Today, it is a festival that celebrates life.

There has been no plague for a very long time, but the Gion Festival still brings the people of Kyoto together to celebrate life with flowers.

The Tea Ceremony

Hayo and Ogino's *ryokan* is not only known for its bouquets: Their mother also specializes in tea ceremonies, or *chanoyu*.

Tea was imported from China by Buddhist monks in the eighth century, and the tea ceremony began to take root in Japan beginning in the twelfth century. Since then, for the majority of Japanese, *chanoyu* is the tradition that best reflects Japanese values: refinement, harmony with nature, aesthetics, art, respect for others, meditation, and philosophy. Considered as one way to attain *wabi*, a state in which you find peace and tranquility through simplicity, the tea ceremony is a true art. For Hayo and Ogino, the *chanoyu* is an important practice during which they feel that they are part a beautiful tradition. They take turns helping their mother to welcome guests and to prepare tea.

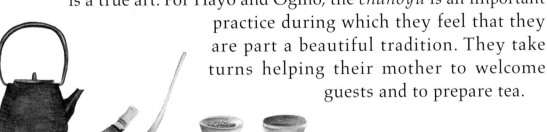

In accordance with tradition, a small pavilion dedicated to the tea ceremony was specially built in the shady part of the *ryokan* garden. The ritual is the same for each ceremony. The guests spend several minutes observing nature in the garden. Then, at the entrance to the pavilion, they take off their shoes. The doorway is particularly small, not higher than two feet—this requires that guests bow when entering. This is a natural way for them to shed their pride and to encourage simplicity. Once inside, they move forward in a kneeling position.

Once all the guests are seated in the formal kneeling position, known as *seiza*, Ogino or Hayo offers small sweet cakes. Then their mother pours hot water into a teapot containing powdered green tea, or *matcha*. Each guest tastes the tea in a ceramic bowl, the *chawan*, and then turns it slightly clockwise three times with the right hand, so that they can admire the different sides of the bowl. When the bowl is empty, each guest turns it in the opposite direction before giving it back to Hayo's mother. She then shows the guests the utensils used to prepare the tea: the spatula, the whisk, and the teapot. This ritual, which is extremely precise, generally takes place in silence in order to encourage meditation.

The tea ceremony, which lasts from thirty to forty minutes, must be a harmonious experience. Many Japanese people hold them at home; sometimes they have several in one day, with different members of their family or friends who have dropped by to visit. Guests are welcomed in a room designed just for this, which is called a *chanoma*.

Like many *ryokan* hosts, Hayo and Ogino's mother must hold several ceremonies in a row. When the small pavilion is empty, Ogino practices greeting her brother. She also wants to become a specialist in the tea ceremony, and in order to do this she must perfect each gesture.

 ## Hayo's Dream: To Become a Sumotori

Hayo loves his country's traditions, and the one that he likes the best is sumo.

In Japan, sumo is a national sport. It is as popular as football is in the United States, or soccer in most of the rest of the world. Every year, six major tournaments are held in Tokyo, Osaka, Nagoya, and Fukuoka.

Hayo and his father go to the one in Osaka, the closest city to Kyoto. Each tournament is a huge event followed by millions of Japanese people. One of Hayo's favorite moments is the opening prefight ceremony, when the *sumotori* (wrestlers) form a circle around the wrestling ring and are presented to the public. Hayo watches them and dreams that one day he will become a *Yokozuna*, the highest rank in sumo.

According to legend, sumo began 2,500 years ago when two gods fought one another for possession of the islands in the Japanese archipelago. At first, sumo matches took place in the villages in order to obtain the blessings of the gods for the coming harvests. Then tournaments were held at more and more places, and wrestlers from all over Japan would pit their strength against each other. It became an official sport in the Heian period (794–1185).

The two sumo wrestlers fight in an area marked by a circle—a kind of ring. Before the fight begins, the *sumotori* face each other and throw salt onto the ring to cleanse all impurities before drinking water from a ladle. Then, each combatant raises a leg to stomp the ground, a symbolic way of crushing any evil spirits that might be nearby. The fight begins at the signal of the referee, who is in the center of the ring. After a period of observation, the wrestlers touch the ground with their hands to accept the combat. Then the fight can begin, and the two *sumotori* charge toward each other. The goal of each wrestler is to either throw his opponent out of the ring or knock him down to the ground. Contrary to its appearance, sumo is a very technical sport.

Sumo, which is based on very specific rules and rituals, is also a very difficult way of life. Hayo already knows that if he wants to become a *sumotori*, he must go to a sumo school after high school. For several years he will live in a sort of commune and train every day with his companions. As a young wrestler, he must also cook, clean, and follow his elders' orders. Finally, he has to gain a lot of weight, because sumo wrestlers must be very strong. In order to do this, he has to eat the same dish, called a *chankonabe*, several times a day. The recipe is kept secret by the sumo masters, and it includes vegetables, meat, and fish. Hayo must also let his hair grow, because sumo wrestlers have to have long hair, slicked back with oil and tied up in a topknot. And, from morning to night and during tournaments, he can only wear a *mawashi*, a piece of fabric wrapped around the waist and between the legs.

Hayo still has time before he can become a sumo wrestler. He must finish high school before going to sumo school. In the meantime, he occasionally tries out his wrestling skills with his best friend, Yukio.

Kenji Lives in Hiroshima: the City of Peace

Kenji is twelve years old. He lives in an apartment with his parents, close to the port of Hiroshima, which is one of the most important parts in Japan. From the balcony outside his room, Kenji can see the enormous bay dotted with small islands.

Even with all the industry that has developed along the bay, there are still lots of small oyster farms. Kenji's grandfather owns several oyster farms and sells his harvest to the restaurants in town. Kenji's father is a taxi driver, and his mother is a secretary for a small clothing company. Kenji's ancestors have always lived in Hiroshima, ever since it was founded several centuries ago.

Hiroshima will always be remembered for the tragedy of August 6, 1945. On that day, the city was destroyed by the first atomic bomb in history. Several days later, a second bomb exploded in Nagasaki, and Japan surrendered to the United States. This tragedy also marked the end of World War II. Years later, the Japanese named Hiroshima the City of Peace, with the prayer that atomic bombs never again be used.

August 6, 1945

The city of Hiroshima, founded by a powerful shogun in the sixteenth century, was a fortified city.

Later, it became an important urban center during the Meiji period, in the second half of the nineteenth century, and then one of the main Japanese military bases in World War I and II. This is why it was the target of American air strikes.

On August 6, 1945, the American bomber *Enola Gay* dropped the first atomic bomb in history, Little Boy. The explosion flattened the city instantly. More than 70,000 buildings and houses were destroyed, and 75,000 people were killed. In the weeks, months, and years that followed, thousands of other people died of complications. More than 250,000 residents of Hiroshima died as a result of the atomic bomb. Three days later, on August 9, 1945, a second atomic bomb was dropped on the city of Nagasaki, where there were thousands more victims.

Kenji's grandfather was seven years old when the atomic bomb was dropped on Hiroshima. He is a *hibakusha*, a bomb survivor. He was very lucky that day: He was exposed to very little radiation because his parents lived on the outskirts of Hiroshima.

Today, he often goes for walks in Peace Memorial Park, which was erected close to the spot where the bomb exploded. Sometimes, he takes Kenji with him to see the Flame of Peace, which burns day and night and will stay lit as long as nuclear weapons continue to exist in the world. One day, when the two of them were walking, Kenji asked him about August 6, 1945.

"Grandfather, what were you doing that day it happened? Were you still asleep?"

"No, I was in our courtyard with my mother, who was hanging laundry. I remember her saying that the sky was strangely quiet. Suddenly, we saw an enormous flash of yellow light, as bright as ten thousand suns. Then a dust cloud rose above the city. It was horrifying. It looked like the end of the world."

"Were you scared?"

"Not at first, because no one knew what had happened. Then we saw hundreds of people leaving the city who were completely deformed. Their clothing was torn, and they walked as best they could just to get out. They didn't know where to go. My mother took in many people because they no longer had anywhere to live. Everything had been destroyed. You can't imagine what a horrible sight it was."

Sadako Sasaki and the One Thousand Cranes

In Peace Memorial Park, there is a monument dedicated to all of the children who were victims of the atomic bomb.

The statue depicts a young girl, Sadako Sasaki, standing on a granite stone and holding a golden crane in her outstretched arms. This crane evokes both a legend and the story of a little girl from Hiroshima. Among the Hiroshima bomb victims were thousands of children, who either died during the explosion, or afterward, when they fell ill with leukemia, a type of cancer, caused by the radiation. Sadako Sasaki is the symbol of these martyrs. She is not only remembered in Peace Memorial Park, but also in schools, like the one Kenji goes to, where a small plaque engraved with Sadako's name hangs in the hallway. Like all Japanese children, Kenji knows her story by heart.

Born in January 1943, Sadako was only two and a half when the atom bomb exploded in Hiroshima. On that day, she was in her room, just a mile from the explosion. Most of her neighbors were killed, but neither Sadako nor her parents were harmed. Years passed, and the little girl grew up normally. She was a very good athlete and an especially fast runner, and she began to participate in competitions.

But one day in 1955—when she was twelve—she suddenly felt extremely tired and dizzy after completing a race. Her parents thought that the vertigo was due to the exhaustion from running. But soon after, she began having other dizzy spells, and one day she collapsed. Her parents took her to the hospital, where she was diagnosed with leukemia, the "atomic bomb disease."

Sadako's best friend, Chizuko, told her the ancient Japanese legend of one thousand cranes. In Japan, the crane is a very important and respected animal because it symbolizes long life. It's said that if you fold one thousand origami cranes, the gods will be pleased and your wish will be granted. Sadako started folding paper cranes immediately, hoping that once she had folded one thousand paper cranes, the gods would cure her disease and let her start running again.

Sadako's family came to visit her in the hospital often, to talk with her and help fold the cranes. After she had folded five hundred, she felt better, and the doctors told her she could go home for a short while. But her dizzy spells began again, and she had to return to the hospital. Sadako spent several months folding a total of 644 paper cranes before she died on October 25, 1955.

Sadako's story spread throughout Hiroshima, and her classmates finished folding the thousand cranes. Then they sold them, and with the money they earned, they built a statue in honor of Sadako and all of the children affected by the atomic bomb. Today, the paper crane is the international symbol of peace. Following Sadako's death, children from across the world began folding cranes and sending them to Hiroshima. Every year in school, Kenji and his classmates spend one day folding dozens of cranes before going to place them in Peace Memorial Park.

Shinto and Zen Buddhism

Like many Japanese, Kenji's family practices both Shinto and Buddhism.

Several months after he was born, Kenji's parents took him to a Shinto priest who blessed him in the name of several gods. "Shinto," which means "The Way of the Gods," is based on the belief in a number of gods or spirits connected to a particular place or natural element, such as Amaterasu, the goddess of the sun. The gods represent the flow of energy that animates the universe and gives life to nature, including plants, rocks, and animals.

Kenji's parents put up a *kamidana* **(shrine)** in the entrance of their apartment to worship the gods. In the middle of the shrine are a miniature Shinto temple and a number of good-luck charms: a small bamboo rake that helps you catch luck, a small red cow made out of papier-mâché to ward off evil, and even a small boat meant to bring treasure. There are

also several small branches of *sakaki*, a sacred tree with the power to attract gods. Kenji often makes a drawing that he places at the foot of the shrine so that the spirits stay for the longest possible time in their apartment.

On New Year's Day, Kenji's family goes to a Shinto temple to pray for the New Year. In the hall designated for making offerings, Kenji places an arrow to which he has attached a piece of paper with a wish written on it. The Japanese say that this arrow has the power to banish evil spirits and grant your wish.

Kenji and his parents also practice Buddhism, which is sometimes considered more of a philosophy than a religion. In Japan, Buddhism and Shinto have become more and more entwined over the years. In the twelfth

century, Zen Buddhism, an offshoot of traditional Buddhism, was brought back from China and began to develop after the creation of five monasteries in Japan. It took on the name *zazen*, which means "to sit in meditation." *Zazen* is a popular practice, and there are thousands of temples throughout Japan. Sometimes, instead of going to a hotel or *ryokan*, some Western tourists spend the night in temples where they can learn *zazen* under the guidance of a master.

Practicing Zazen

Kenji and his father go to a temple two nights a week to practice *zazen*. This is common in Japan, not only among Zen Buddhists, but also among those who seek some form of spiritual training.

Zazen is a philosophy and an art of meditation. In English, the word "Zen" is sometimes used to mean "detachment" or "serenity"; it is a synonym for the word "calm."

When Kenji and his father enter the temple, they greet the people present by putting their palms together and bowing slightly, out of respect. Then they sit on the floor, with the monks and other Buddhists like them. Sometimes there are even foreign tourists. Kenji's father taught him how to sit and breathe correctly at home. At the temple, a teacher helps him master this. Knowing how to sit and breathe correctly are two things that are very important in *zazen*.

Kenji sits cross-legged in the lotus position, with his right foot on his left thigh and his left foot on his right thigh. His knees touch the ground and he must sit very straight, as if he were pushing on the ground with his knees and up toward the sky with his head. Then he closes his eyes slightly. His left hand rests on his right hand, the palms facing upward. Each detail is important because all parts of the body are connected and affect one another. The body must be totally stable in order to focus on meditation.

The most important part of *zazen* is breathing. There are several techniques. Kenji learned the simplest one, called *shoshuten*: He inhales deeply and follows his breath moving up his spine until it reaches the spot between his eyes. He holds his breath and imagines a

warm light, such as the sun. Kenji then exhales slowly and starts over. It is not long before his breathing is calm, powerful, and natural.

Sometimes, when Kenji is meditating, a master or assistant strikes him lightly on the right shoulder with the *jikido* (the sword of wisdom) to indicate that he is sitting incorrectly. In silence, he adjusts his posture and begins meditating again, trying not to think about anything else. As his father says, *zazen* has no goal. It simply helps you to become more peaceful. After each session, Kenji has the feeling that his spirit is as clear as a cloudless sky.

The Game of Go
and the Spirit of Japanese Philosophy

Kenji wanted to learn to play *go* ever since reading a *manga* about Hikaru, a boy of his age.

One day, Hikaru finds an old *go* board, or *goban*, in his attic. He thinks it is particularly beautiful and decides to take it down to his room. Soon after, Hikaru learns that the board is possessed by a mysterious ghost named Sai, an ancient *go* master who taught an emperor in the Heian period, in approximately 850. The ghost makes Hikaru play *go*, teaching him the best moves. Sometime later at a tournament, Hikaru faces the talented Akira and beats him. From this point on, a great rivalry develops between the two players. Each one tries to learn the best strategies in order to become the best *go* master. Hikaru is helped by the ghost Sai, who has been searching for the "divine move" for more than one thousand years. Fascinated by Hikaru's story, Kenji immediately wanted to learn to play *go* in a club.

According to legend, *go* was invented more than four thousand years ago by two Chinese emperors, Yao and Shun, who wanted to impart wisdom to their sons at an early age. In fact, *go* is one of the oldest games in the world. At first, *go* was only played at the emperor's court, but later, *go* schools were founded throughout Japan. *Go* masters were very

respected, and profited from special privileges in the shogun's courts. The Japanese like to say that *go* perfectly embodies the spirit of their philosophy. Actually, the game of *go* represents a way of life. It demands enormous mental discipline and long reflection, and is hugely popular. It is a complex, sophisticated game of strategy.

The first time that Kenji found himself in front of the neighborhood club's *go* board, he was in awe. For one hour, an old master patiently explained to him the basic rules of the game. He told him that the two players must alternately place their black or white stones, or pieces, on the board, and the player who wins is the one whose stones control a larger territory than his or her opponent's. But the bigger the territory, the harder it is to protect it from an opponent's attacks.

In *go*, there is no second place. At the end of the match, the winner is the one who, capable of blending attack and defense, has successfully expanded his or her own territory and reduced that of the opponent. The loser is the one who recklessly set out to conquer an area without having found a way to defend it.

After one hour of explanations and demonstrations, Kenji felt ready to play his first game. The old master, who has taught thousands of players in his life, explained to him that impatience is normal, because, after an hour of explanations, everyone thinks he or she knows how to play *go*. But he told Kenji that even one lifetime would not be enough to master the game. Kenji understood this only several minutes into the first game. Before he even had time to realize what happened, the old master's white stones surrounded his black stones, which could no longer move.

When he came for his second class, Kenji learned that *go* is not a game of chance and that luck plays no part. Like his hero, Hikaru, Kenji has begun to learn different strategies. Today, in spite of his young age, Kenji is already respected in the club. Like the ghost Sai, his secret dream is to one day discover the "divine move."

Photography Credits:

p. 5: copyright © Orion Press/Stone/Getty Images
p. 7: copyright © Bob Rowan; Progressive Image/Corbis
p. 9: All rights reserved
p. 11: copyright © Michael S. Yamashita/Corbis
p. 12: copyright © Tom Wagner/Corbis
p. 19: copyright © Akg-Images
p. 20–21: copyright © Ed Freeman/Getty Images
p. 23: All rights reserved
p. 25: copyright © Sam Clemens/Digital Vision/Getty Images
p. 30: copyright © Hulton Archive/Getty Images
p. 32: copyright © Kharbine-Tapabor/Coll. S. Kakou
p. 35: All rights reserved
p. 36: copyright © Akg-Images
p. 38: copyright © Akg-Images
p. 41: copyright © Akg-Images/Suzanne Held
p. 46: copyright © Hulton Archive/Getty Images

Library of Congress Cataloging-in-Publication Data:
Messager, Alexandre.
[Aoki, Hayo et Kenji vivent au Japon. English.]
We live in Japan / by Alexandre Messager ; illustrations by
Sophie Duffet.
p. cm. — (Kids around the world)
ISBN-13: 978-0-8109-1283-0
ISBN-10: 0-8109-1283-X
1. Japan—Juvenile literature 2. Children—Japan—Juvenile
literature. I. Duffet, Sophie. II. Title.
DS806.M47 2007
952—dc22
2006023101

Copyright © 2006 Éditions de la Martinière, Paris
Translated by Christopher Pitts
English translation copyright © 2007 Harry N. Abrams, Inc.

Printed and bound in France
by Pollina - n° L42145d
10 9 8 7 6 5 4 3 2 1

HNA ▪▪▪▪▪
harry n. abrams, inc.
a subsidiary of La Martinière Groupe
115 West 18th Street
New York, NY 10011
www.hnabooks.com